MACBOOK

SENIORS GUIDE

THE COMPLETE, EASY-TO-FOLLOW ILLUSTRATED MANUAL
TO MASTER YOUR MACBOOK AIR AND PRO.

LEARN ALL THE FEATURES IN LESS THAN 7 DAYS
WITH EASY & STEP-BY-STEP INSTRUCTIONS.

HENRY SANDERS

TABLE OF CONTENTS

ALPHABETICAL INDEX

T

U

Y

INTRODUCTION

With all the choices out there, you might be asking yourself "why choose a MacBook?" If we were to make a list on all the reasons what sets a MacBook aside from all the other laptops on the market it would be very long. But to name a few: first things first, MacBook is actually ranking on the catalog when talking about which one is the best laptop for new-users and seniors to buy. It is easy to access and meets all the basic needs of everyone. The consistency and the logical nature of the processor of a MacBook makes it easier for a non-tech-savvy to get immediately familiarized with the computer. Not to mention that, if you already have an iPhone, or an iPad or any other Apple device, you can easily connect it to your MacBook and have the main futures such as phone calls and iMessages running from your MacBook when you are using it. Yes, a big deterrent might be the price, but in the long wrong it is actually the cheaper option. MacBooks' values actually run and stay stable for a longer time confronted to many other up-front laptops, and its life expectancy is quite stunning. When surfing through the internet it is just a matter of one click to stumble into a virus, this is an issue that a lot of other laptops, such as Windows, have to deal with far more than apple run MacBooks. If you want both the worlds you still can run Windows on a MacBook by downloading the correct program, the same can not be said about a Windows laptop. The whole products is built by Apple, from the hardware design to the very last chips, which makes the overall experience smoother. A normal pc pieces is typically ensembled by different manufacturers. The limited number of available types of

MacBooks actually makes it easier to purchase the right one for your needs, that will hit all the right spots in terms of functionality. Sometimes, when it comes to regular pcs, it's easy to get confused by the wide variety available, and it's even easier to end up buying the wrong laptop for you.

In this book you will find a complete guide on how to get started with your MacBook and how to get more familiarized with this technology to getting to know some tricks and tips that will come in handy when using your MacBook. To make it even easier, you will find everything in an alphabetical order, without having to waste time or energy going through the whole book in attempt to find the right topic for you. But the help is not over yet, at the end of the book you will also find a little summary on the terminologies used throughout the book that will help you understand better what you are actually dealing with and looking at.

Now let's get started!

THE BASIS

COMPONENTS OF YOUR MAC

Familiarize first with the components and the ports of your MacBook.

All MacBooks come with built in ports that are designed to connect any external hard-drive or USB-drives, to charge your Mac, no matter what model you have, you will use the charger that can be as the regular one, one piece. (Like the picture below)

Or in two separate pieces, a wall charger and its usb cord. (See picture below)

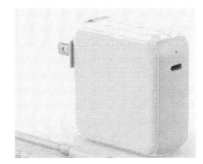

First time turning on your Mac

Open your Mac, if doesn't turn on, on the top right-hand side there will be a button with the power sign on, (newer versions come in as a blank button), press down on it in order to turn on your MacBook. Once it is turned on you can get started setting up your Mac.

Circled in the picture below is the button to press in order to turn on your MacBook on latest models.

Circled in the picture below is the button to be pressed in order to turn on your MacBook on previous models.

Sleep and Wake up button

When you are not using your MacBook the best way to save battery is to set it up to automatically go "to sleep". Turning on and off your MacBook actually takes longer than letting it go to sleep and waking it up once you are ready to use it again. Here are the steps to follow:

1. Select the Apple menu (which is the apple icon on the top left of the screen)
2. Scroll down on the pop up window and select the voice "Sleep"

- Another way is to simply close the lid of your MacBook, which automatically puts it to sleep.

To wake up your Mac simply do one of the following steps:

1. If you simply shut down the lid of the Mac all you have to do is reopen it, the system will automatically turn back on itself.
2. Press on the keyboard any key or move your mouse.

A great feature is also the fact that you can schedule the time you want your MacBook to shut down – turn on, go to sleep – or wake up. This is the best solution when you want to make sure your MacBook is not running when you are nota round.

1. Choose the Apple menu
2. Click on System Preferences
3. Select the voice "Energy Saver"
4. The select the voice "Schedule".

From here you can choose the option you want to customize, whether it's the time frame you want your MacBook to shutdown or simply go to sleep. Once you have choosen the time, from the pop-up menu remember to always click Apply, so that the changes will be saved and applied in the future.

When you first turn on your MacBook you will be asked to choose your language preference, which will be used to run your MacBook. Select the language you want to use and then click the arrow on the corner.

Second step will be asking you your country Region.

The third page will be asking you the accessibility you want to enable, to help you have a better experience. For instance, if you have any troubles with your vision or hearing you can choose the two icons to setup the features that will help you have an easier time with your Mac.

Next step will be asking you to setup your WiFi, so if you are in the comfort of your house you can select your network and connect your MacBook.

Next will be a disclaimer on your Data and Privacy while using your MacBook, from which you can choose and control what you want to share or not.

This next step, as it tells its own name, will let you migrate your files from a previous computer. So if you were already using an Apple product before (files, datas and settings), you can migrate your files to your new MacBook either through your WiFi, and the same thing can be done from a Windows laptop (in this case only your datas).

If you are a brand-new user, you can simply click on the "Not now" title, which can be found on the bottom left corner.

Next step will be setting your Apple ID, if you already have one you simply just have to type in your credentials. If you don't have one yet, you can easily set it up by clicking on create new Apple ID. It is essential for you to create an Apple ID in order to be able to use the Mac to its fullest potential.

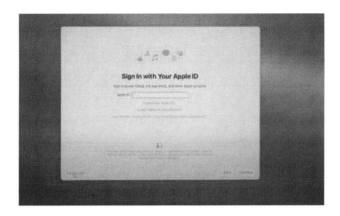

Once you have accepted the terms and conditions, the next screen will ask you to set a user name and password for your user account. Some times there might be more than one user of the same MacBook, creating your Computer Account comes in handy when you want to keep files and datas separated between you and the other user (s).

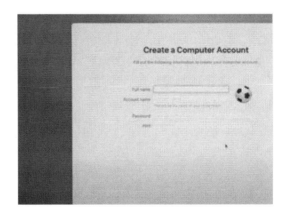

This window will give you the option so Set Up your MacBook according to the default options, but if you already have in mind a specific set up you can simply click on "Customize Settings" option on the bottom left, in order to be able to customizeyour options. (For example locations, analytics information, screen time and the time you spend on your MacBook, setting up Siri)

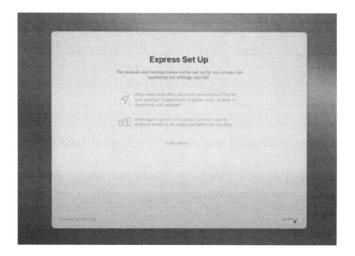

Touch ID

This particular feature, very similar to the one available on the iPhones and iPads, allows you to unlock your Mac, authorize purchases by simpling pressing on the button. You can choose to set it up the first time you are setting up your Mac, or letter.

If you choose to set it up from the beginning these are the steps to be followed.

This first window will appear on your screen, click on "continue"

You will be guided through the whole process through pop up windows that will tell you what to do.

You can choose which ever finger you prefer, and gently tap on the power button (as shown on the picture above) several times, by lifting and taping again on the very same button. Make sure to also get the edges of your finger.

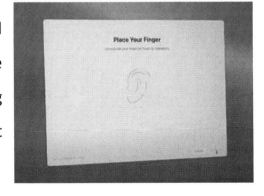

Once your MacBook has acquired your fingerprint, you will be notified that the Touch ID is ready, at this point, simply click on "continue".

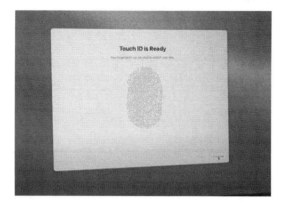

Once you have set your laptop it will apply all the settings you have chosen (which can take up to a few minutes) and redirect you to the Desktop.

Desktop

Once you have done setting everything up, and every time you will use your MacBook, your Desktop will be the first thing you will see. The desktop is sort of a virtual desk, a starting point, from where you can access documents, files, data, surf the internet, ecc.

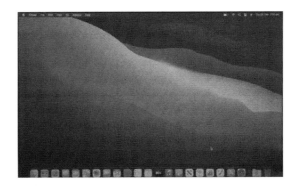

To make it easy, we can divide the desktop into three major parts.

The Menu Bar (above), the main desk where or better yet Window, where your windows will appear. For example, if you open Safari, the page will appear on the middle and widest part of the screen. And lastly, the Dock. You can imagine ita s a sort of drawer of your actual desk, from which you can pull up all sorts of things such as a notebook pad, your contacts, calendars and much more.

Finder

 This icon can be found at the bottom left side of you dock. Once you click on this icon a pop up window will show up (like the one shown below).

Finder is where you can find all the apps, data, files, and more, that are inside of your computer, through which you can manage and organize all of your files, which will help you save time trying to find where one specific file was saved.

How do you use finder?

On the top of the window you can find the toolbar.

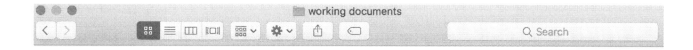

On the left side you have the sidebar.

If you are searching for something specif, that you are having a hard time finding, simply type a key word (for example: grocery list) on the search bar, which can be found on the top righ corner of the toolbar.

What you can do from Finder is also gain easy access to different folders. For example, you have recently downloaded an app, but you can't find it on your desktop. All you have to do is click on "Application" on the sidebar, and all your applications will show on the window.

Dock

As already mentioned earlier, the dock can be find at the bottom of the desktop.

On the dock you will find several icons that if clicked will automatically redirect you to the specific application.

The dock can be rearranged, meaning you can add, move or delete applications. But let's go by order.

On the left corner you will find the "recycle bin" where your deleted files will be sent, and from where you can retrieve any data in case you change your mind. Next to the "recycle bin", you will find the download folder, where you can access all the documents you have downloaded.

Download

Folder   Recycle bin

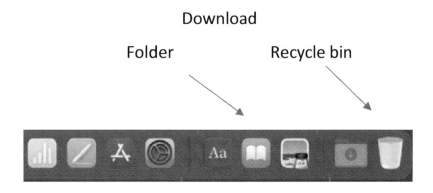

When you have multiple windows running on the background, your MacBook, gives you easy and quicker access to them by adding their icon between the Download folder and the rest of the apps. (See the picture below for reference)

In this case we have three application that have been used recently and they are separated from the applications by a line.

How to move /add apps on the dock

1. To add an item on the dock you simply have to drag the app into the dock.
2. To remove an item from the dock simply drag the icon out of the dock until "Remove" appears. The app will still be on your laptop, the only that will be erased is the icon from the dock.
3. To move an icon simply click on the icon and drag it around the dock until it reaches the position desired.

Menu-bar

1   2

The menu bar can be found on the top of the screen. From here you can run commands, carry out tasks.

1. If clicked you can find the most important settings and funcionality of the system, i.e: information about your computer, access to the App Store, recently used folders.

2. The options "Font Book", "File", "Edit", "View", "Window", and "Help" are part of the app menu. The app menu refers to the actions you can take regarding the application currently opened or being used. When there is an app opened the following options of "File", "Edit", "View", "Window" will appear.

3. The "Help" option will always be available on the menubar, whether there is an opened application currently being used, or not.

The second part of the menu-bar is the status menus. (Right end of the menu bar). On this side of the bar you can customize features such as: turning ON and OFF the Wi-Fi, volume, battery status, time and date.

1. 🔍 "Spotlight" icon, by clicking on the icon you may run all kinds of researches that will give you results that are both from you Mac and the web.

2. 🎛 "Control Center", similar to the one that can be found for example on iPhone or iPad, through this icon you can have access to the features you use more often for example: AirPlay, Bluetooth, AirDrop, ecc.

3. ⚪ The Siri may be included on the menu bar, although not always, by clicking on this icon you can use Siri to do task such as open files or find files or surf the internet for a specific topic.

Activate your Wi-Fi

To connect your MacBook to the WiFi you can:

1. 📶 You can click on the WiFi menu that can be found on the menubar. A pop up menu window will appear. Make sure your WiFi is on, if the bar next to "Wi-Fi" appears to be blue then your Wi-Fi is on. From this pop up menu window a list of the available Wi-Fi will appear, from which you can choose yours. Remember, if required, you may be asked to insert also the Wi-Fi's password.

Another way to connect your MacBook to the Wi-Fi, if the icon is not available on the menu bar, you can simply

1. click on the Apple menu
2. select "System Preferences"
3. select "Network"
4. click on "Wi-Fi"
5. finally select "Show Wi-Fi status in the menu bar"

By following these steps the Wi-Fi icon will appear on your menu bar and you will be able to connect your computer to the Wi-Fi connection, and have a quick and easy access to the Wi-Fi feature.

Activate the right click of your mouse

What is the right click of the mouse? Apple computer products are known to have only one click available mouse. If you have ever owned a Windows laptop you are familiar with the right button on the mouse, which allowed you to have access to further features. This characteristic on the MacBook can be done through the double click. Actually, you can activate the right click on you MacBook, the steps to follow are the following:

1. Select the "Menu Apple"
2. Click on "System Preferences"
3. Choose "Trackpad"
4. Select the folder "Point & Click"
5. Select "Secondary Click". A pop up menu will appear from which you can choose the type of click, in this case "Click in bottom right corner"

Smart zoom

Besides the regular method of zooming, if you have a Magic Mouse or a Magic Trackpad you can also use the smart zoom feature.

Magic mouse	Magic Trackpad

This function allows you to zoom in an specific point of the page through a simple touch. To activate this feature simply follow as listed below:

1. Go to "System Preferences"

a. If you are using your magic mouse click on "Mouse"
b. Click on "Point and click"
c. Make sure that the bar next to the title "Smart Zoom" is on, if it's off simply click on it as it switches to the blue color.

a. If you are using your Magic Trackpad go to "System Preferences"
b. Click on "Trackpad"
c. Select "Scroll and zoom"
d. Make sure the bar net to the title "Smart Zoom" is on, if it's off simply click on it as it switches to the blue color.

Control Center

The control center gives you easy and immediate accesso to some features such as screen brightness, volume, Wi-Fi connection and other functions that normally would be adjustable through the "System Preferences". This feature is the very same that can be found on devices such as iPads and iPhones. This characteristic is available on macOS11.

As already mentioned earlier, the control center is on the menu bar, you can access to it by simply clicking on the icon .

Once selected this menu will appear:

Unlike the other Apple's devices, the control center can be personalized only to a certain extent. You can add other applications in order to have a quicker shortcut, to do so simply follow the below listed steps:

1. Open "System Preferences"

2. Click on "Dock and Menu bar"

3. On the left, under the title "Contro Center" you can access to all the features available and choose whether you want them to appear or not, but you can not delete them.

There are different applications that can be used to navigate online, Safari is the default application when using an Apple product. To run the program you will simply have to click on the icon, which is normally found on the dock.

Once you have opened Safari, the main page will appear, which usually appears to be like the following:

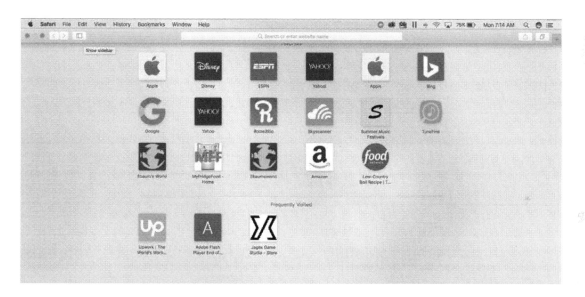

You will notice that on the left corner side of the menu bar more options will appear, such as:

➤ Bookmarks, where you can find all the internet pages you have saved to be revised at a later time.

➢ History, where you can access and check all the researches that have been done on the Internet on your MacBook.

Marked in green are the options to close, minimize or hide the page.

➢ If the red button is clicked you will close the page. Sometimes it may happen that by clicking the red button you are actually just closing the page you are actually still running on the app. To completely close the app you can click on, for example in this case, "Safari" on the app menu and from the option window click on quit.

➢ If the yellow button is clicked the page will be "shrunk" to the Dock, but you will still be running on the same application.

➢ The green button, which is the full screen button. Once clicked it will open the page on the entire screen.

These rules do not only apply when using Safari, but they extend to all the other applications of the MacBook, when being used.

Highlighted in light blue you will find suggestions of pages and links that your MacBook detects and suggest to you that might be of your interest.

Safari's Functions

Safari's function is mainly related to the Internet and web searching.

1. To begin your research simply type in a few keywords on the search bar, which can be found at the top center of the page. For example, if you are looking for news simply type "news".

2. Another way to make researches is to first type google on the search bar

   The google main page will appear from which you can make your researches by typing on the search bar.

➢ On the top left corner you will notice these arrows:

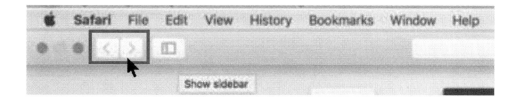

These arrows will allow you to move back and forward in between the Internet pages you have visited in this session.

> To use multiple tabs while on Safari you can do it by clicking on the plus icon that is on the right top corner. By doing this a new tab will be available where you can make a second research.

To navigate in between tabs simply click on the one you want to access to. You can also rearrange the positions by pressing and dragging the tab to the position you prefer.

In order to close one of the multiple tabs hoover above the tab and then click on the "X" button.

> To view all your tabs at once click on the doble square at the top right corner

> If you find yourself on a website that you often visit or would like to save for a later time, you can save the site by using the Bookmark. This way you will have easy access to the page without having to enter the link again. To do so click on the share icon on the top right

From here you will have the option to add the page on a
bookmark. From the window that will appear you can assign
where to put your bookmark.

To find all the pages you have saved through bookmark you will have to click on the
book icon that can be found at the top left of the browser's page

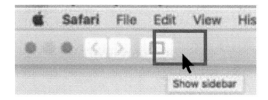

Once clicked a side will appear where you can scroll through all the pages you have
saved.

Another way is to simply click on "Bookmarks" menu at the top.

Add an e-mail account to your MacBook

 If you happen to have multiple email accounts, to add them simply follow as listed below:

1. Access on the e-mail by clicking on its icon

2. From the menu bar select "Mail"

3. From the options click on "Add Account"

4. From the pop up window select your provider. For example: seniorsguide@gmail.com (the email ending in gmail will have Google as a provider).

5. You will be guided through on the desk to enter your new account's details.

Add a printer

There are several ways to add a printer to your MacBook according to the type of the printer you have, here we will cover the main two methods that are used.

Wireless Printer

Wireless printers do not need to be connected to the computer through a USB chord, the printer connects to the MacBook through the "Wi-Fi".

Make first sure your printer is connected to the "Wi-Fi" and then from your computer:

1. Click the Apple icon on the top left corner of your screen.
2. From the pop up menu select "System Preferences"
3. Select "Printers and Scanners "
4. On the page click on the + icon
5. From the menu select the printer you wish to add
6. Click "Add"

Add a printer through a USB chord

1. Plug the printer to the computer through the USB chord
2. Click the Apple icon on the top left corner of your screen
3. From the pop up menu select "System Preferences"
4. Select "Printers and Scanners"
5. Click the + sign on the page
6. From the menu select the printer you wish to add
7. Click "Add"

Apple ID

An apple ID is essential when it comes to using an Apple device, especially because it allows you to have access to the iTunes Store, App Store, FaceTime and all the other services provided by Apple.

To create an Apple ID

1. Click on the apple icon
2. Select System Preferences
3. Click on "Sign in"
4. On the page that will appear, create first your email address my typing on the Apple ID bar. For example Senior.guide
5. Once you have typed in the email address click on "Create Apple ID"
6. Enter your credit card and billing address then choose "Continue", you can also choose to "None" and add a payment menthod at a later time.

To add an already existing Apple ID (if you did not log in during the configuration):

1. Choose the Apple log on the upper left corner
2. Select "System Preferences"
3. Click on "Sign In"
4. Enter your credentials

Crop, copy and paste

If you are switching from a Windows to a MacBook, it might be confusing because on MacBook in order to crop, copy or paste you will need to use the shortcuts on the keyboard, here they are:

How to copy

If there is a text you want to copy from one file to the other:

1. Highlight the text you are interested to
2. Press "Command+C"

How to crop

By cropping or cutting an object or text from a file you are actually going to cut this piece of information so that it won't appear anymore on the original document:

1. Highlight the text
2. Press "Command+X"

How to paste

Now that you have the object or text you want to move, to paste it in the new document:

➢ Press "Command+V"

Apple Store App

 The Apple Store application, just as on any other Apple device, gives you a quick access online to all the products and services that the company offers to its customers.

The application is usually found on the dock.

If you are looking to download a specific application

1. simply click on the icon
2. on the left side type in the search bar the application, for example "Facebook"
3. click on the button "Get" to initiate the download.

If instead of the "Get" option appears a number, for example, $1,20, then you will have to pay the amount reported in order to obtain the application.

Air Drop

 The Air Drop function allows you to quickly share and transfer files between Apple device. Air Drop uses either Bluetooth or Wi-Fi connection to transfer files.

Before you begin make sure you check these boxes

1. Both devices are close to each other withing a Bluetooth or Wi-Fi range.
2. Make sure either Bluetooth or Wi-Fi are turned ON on both device, according to which one you are going to use to transfer the files
3. To share between one device to another make sure they appear in each other's Contacs or have either the email address or phone number.

To Air Drop from your Mac:

1. Open the file you wish to share
2. Click on the shar button
3. From the pop up menu select "AirDrop"
4. Choose the contact you wish to send the file to

To receive something through Air drop:

Whenever someone is attempting to share with you through Air drop, you will receive a notification asking if you either want to accept or decline the file. On the same window you will also be able to see the person sending who's sending you the file.

All the files that you receive through Air Drop can be found in the "Downloads" folder.

Spotlight

 What is Spotlight? Spotlight is a convenient way to find applications, folders, files on your MacBook.

1. You can use it by clicking on the magnifying icon on the top of your screen.

Q Spotlight Search

This pop-up bar will appear, and you can type in the folder, application, or file you are looking for.

2. You can press on "Command + Space"

What is great about using Spotlight is that this type of search combines all the findings from the research in one place.

Siri

 In order to access Siri you can use the icon in the Menu Bar, you can also access it in the Touch Bar (on MacBooks Pro).

What can Siri do?

The primary and most obvious function for Siri is to gather information, for example "What is the weather going to be in Atlanta, tomorrow?". You can click on the results that will redirect you to the appropriate page to have more information, i.e. a website page.

Once Siri is opened, to close it, you can click on the "X" button, or it will automatically close on its own once you start doing other tasks.

To ask another question you can click on the button , that appears at the bottom of the pop-up page.

You can ask Siri to also carry out some simple task on your Mac, for example launching some apps, open files, search the web for a specific topic.

You can schedule events, for example "schedule a meeting for Friday at 2 o'clock. Send e-mails, messages, FaceTime.

To personalize the settings of your Siri you can do so by

1. clicking on the Apple icon on the top left corners
2. select "System Preferences"
3. from the menu select the "Siri" icon

From this page you can turn and off Siri by checking on the box "Enable Ask Siri",

Change the keyboard shortcut, language, and much more.

Notification

The notification on MacBook appears on the upper right-hand corner of the desk.

Once they disappear you can access them once again by clicking on the date and time on the upper right corner.

Once you have opened your notification center, you can choose to dismiss a certain notification by simply clicking on the "X" button. Depending on the type of application that the notification is coming from you have other options, for example, in the example used above you have the "Snooze" option because it's coming from the "Calendar" application.

If you are getting too many notifications, you can control the amount of notification you get by:

1. Click on the left top corner on the Apple iconSelect "System Preferences"
2. Select "Notifications"

You will see a list menu of applications that are using the notification feature, you can select on any of them to access the option to disable the notification for that specific application.

On the "System Preferences, Notification" you can also select the "Do Not Disturb" option

This option will allow you to choose the hours in which you do not want to get notifications.

For example, in between certain hours, or when your laptop is off.

A quicker way to turn on the "Do Not Disturb" feature is by clicking on the notification center and click on the "Do Not Disturb" box. This way you will not get notification on the desktop, but your notification will still be available on the "Notification Center".

Apple pay

Apple pay allows you to make purchases on website that are approved by Apple Pay. In order to use this feature, besides having a Credit or Debit card, your computer has to have the "Touch ID". To set up your Apple Pay on your computer:

1. Select the Apple icon on the left corner of your screen
2. Choose "System Preferences"
3. Click on "Wallet & Apple Pay"
4. Click "Add Card": you can use the card you have entered while setting up your Apple ID or select to add a new card as a method of payment.

Now that you have your "Apple pay" set up, all you have to do to use this payment method is choose "Apple pay" next time you are checking out from an online store, or place your finger on your Touch ID to complete the transaction.

Rename files

To rename a file on your MacBook there are several ways to accomplish this task.

First way:

1. Select the file

2. On the "File" menu select the option "Rename"

Second way:

1. Select the file

2. Press the return button on your keyboard

3. Rename the file

Rename multiple files at the same time:

1. Select all files

2. Click on "File" menu

3. Select "Rename"

How to change the name of your MacBook

To change the name of your Mac, which is the name used when carrying out tasks lie file sharing, follow the instructions:

1. Click on the Apple logo on the top corner of your screen
2. Select "System Preferences"
3. Select "Sharing" from the menu
4. At the top of the page you will see the name of your computer, from which you can change the name by simply typing in the bar.

Screen Time feature

This feature tracks your time of usage of the applications on your computer and allows you to restrict the amount of time used on your computer, which can come handy when you want to set up a parental control. To access to screen time:

1. Select the Apple logo from the top left corner of your screen
2. Click "System Preferences"
3. On the menu select "Screen Time"

From the page you will see the data that your MacBook has gathered from your usage of your laptop. By default it gives you the data of the last day, but you can change the filters and select the days you are looking for. You will get a list of the applications used and the time spent on those applications.

Remember, that if an application is open but not being used, your MacBook is still going to track the time the time since the application is still running.

To set your parental control:

➢ You can set the "Downtime" and choose specific time frames where the computer should not be used at all. During the "Down time' you will be able to use only the application you set on the "Always Allowed" list.

➢ From "App limits" you can select a specific application to set on limits. For example: you can allow the keynote app only for a specific amount of time. Once you have set a limit time to an application and you reach the threshold this will appear on your screen

You can click on "Ok" to close the application or "Ignore Limit" to give yourself more time. This can be done on an administrator account, all other accounts on the MacBook will not get the ability to over run the limitation.

➢ From "Content and Privacy" if turned on you can limit the content, for example, adults websites.

Battery percentage

By default your MacBook will always show you the state of your battery. The battery level will decrease as you are using your computer and will alert you when the battery is too low before your MacBook turns off. A very useful feature is the possibility of having the actual percentage to appear beside the battery logo, that way you can plan ahead instead of waiting to be "alerted" by your computer. To enable this feature:

1. Click on the Apple logo at the top left side corner of your screen
2. Select "System Preferences"
3. Select "Dock & Menu Bar" from the menu
4. Slide down to the bottom and select "Battery" option
5. Select "Show Percentage"

You will see that the percentage will appear next to the battery logo on the Menu bar.

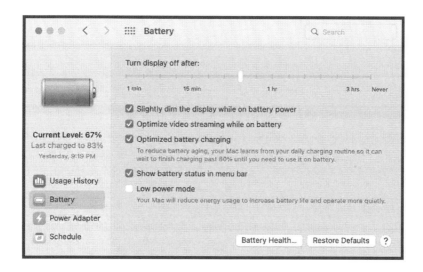

Customize volume and alert notification

When you are watching a video, listening to music, or doing task that requires the use of the speaker of your laptop, there are two ways you can customize the volume of your MacBook.

First, if you are using an application such as YouTube, you can customize the volume directly from the app. Sometimes, even if the application's volume is at the highest level, this might still not be enough. In this case, you can apply a higher volume by directly customizing the volume coming out of your speakers. There are three buttons on your keyboard.

This button when pressed will mute or unmute your speakers 	These two buttons will allow you to turn up or down your volume, according to your preference. 

Your computer will also give you sound alerts when it comes to notifications, incoming call, when you are trying to do something that you are not allowed to, ecc.

To set your alert sound:

1. Click on the Apple logo from the top left corner of your screen
2. Select "System Preferences"
3. Select "Sound" from the menu

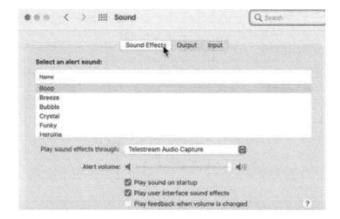

4. From this menu select "Sound Effects"
5. And you can choose the type of alert sound you prefer from the menu.

Date and Time on your menu bar

To change the time or date shown on the menu bar of your computer:

1. Click on the apple logo on the top left corner of your screen

2. Select "System Preferences"

3. From the menu select "Date & Time"

   a. You can choose automatically and the only thing you have to make sure is to select the correct, region or time zone.
   b. You can input the date and time manually by turning off "Set date and time automatically", then select the correct date on the calendar and drag the clock to the correct time.

4. Click "Save"

5. Select your time zone:

   a. Automatically, which uses the location that your laptop is sharing
   b. Manually by turning off "Set time zone automatically using correct location", click on the location on the map.

The time and date on your menu bar should always appear in a manner that is easy to read, but it can happen that the characters result to be dull or grey, which makes it harder to read (see picture below for reference)

This happens because your computer may be running on "Do Not Disturb" mode. This because you might have set a "Do Not Disturb" time frame prior. The date and time will appear back to normal once your computer will not be in this mode either automatically or manually because you have decided to turn off the "Do Not Disturb" mode.

Drag and drop

Drag and drop allows you to move an item within a folder or from folder to folder. The most basic way to drag and drop is simply done by:

1. Click on the file, continue to press the mouse or the track pad
2. Move the pointer to the new position
3. Release the finger from the button and the item will move the new designated area

To select multiple items to drag and drop, that are not close to each other:

1. Select your first file and press without releasing the Command key button
2. Select the other items
3. Release the command key button
4. Move your pointer to the new location selected

To select multiple files that are in the same row or a consequently one after the other:

1. Move your pointer in space where there is no item
2. Click and drag the rectangle above the files you want to move (remember they have to be consequently one after the other, for example a row of 5 files, or 3 rows of 15 files). All the files that will be under the rectangle will be selected.
3. Once you have all the files under the rectangle drag and drop the files to the new location desired.

Install and Uninstall Applications on your MacBook

As we have already covered in the previous chapters, you can install application by going on the App Store and downloading the application you are looking for. If you decided to uninstall an application, this is the proper way to do so:

1. Launch the "Launchpad", that can be found on the dock
2. All your applications will appear on your screen
3. Click and hold on any application
4. All the applications will start to wiggle showing an "X" on the left corner of each icon
5. Click the "X"

Some of the applications might not show an "X" this because the application might be part of the operating system, so it is necessary to run your computer, so they can not be deleted. Another reason why the "X" might not appear is because the application was not downloaded from the App Store, for example "Whats App" has to be downloaded from the official website page.

To uninstall an application that was not downloaded from the App Store, therefore is not showing an "X":

1. Click on "Go" from the menu bar
2. From the menu click on "Applications"
3. From the list find the application you wish to uninstall
4. Select and drag it to the trash bin on the dock in order to delete it

*It is common that, when scrolling through the Apple Store or searching the Internet, you might come across an application that is supposed to clean your MacBook (delete applications). Do not trust this applications as they usually do not do the intended task and most likely will be doing harm to your computer, such as viruses.

Quit Force Unresponsive Applications

Sometimes your application may freeze and will stop running and are taking too long to start running again. In this case the best solution is to quit the application and restart it. Unfortunately, unless the application is set to save every changes automatically, if you have not saved the file, prior to the application being unresponsive, all updates will be lost. Here are the steps to follow:

1. Click on the Apple logo on the left upper corner of your screen
2. Select "Force Quit" from the menu option
3. Select the application you wish to force quit
4. Click on "Force Quit" at the bottom right corner
5. Click on "Force Quit" from the pop up window, to give your confirmation

Moving and resizing windows open on your screen

We already know that there are specific buttons to "hide/minimize" or widen a window. But you can actually customize the size of the window you are working on.

1. Move your pointer to the edges of the window

2. Your pointer will change shape (picture for reference)

3. The edge right or left if you want to make it wider or smaller

- If you do it from the left or right edge you will customize the width of the window

- If you do it from the bottom or top of the edge you will customize how big the window will look

- You can resize the window by also dragging from any of the window's corners.

Other tricks to know when it comes to resizing a window:

❖ Bring your pointer to the right side of the window and double click, this will expand the window to the edge of the screen. This can be done on any side of the window.

❖ Double click on any corner the clicked corner to the edge of the screen. For example, if you double click on the right corner it will expand it to the edge of the right corner of the screen.

❖ Hold the "Option" key on your keyboard and bring your pointer either to the right or left edge of the window to resize both sides at the same time. Same steps can be followed also either for the top or bottom edge.

❖ Press "Shift" button on the keyboard and drag one edge, this will resize three sides of the window.

❖ Press "Option" key button and double click either on the right or left side to move both sides towards the edges of the screen at the same time. The same steps can be followed both for the top and the bottom.

❖ Press "Option" key button and double click on any of the corner of the window to move all four sides at the same time.

To move a window, when you have multiple windows opened:

1. Move your pointer on the edges of the window, make sure you are not above any option

2. Drag the window to where you want to locate it on the screen

How to create a folder

 As you download applications, add files, etc., it is best to learn how to create new folders so that you can keep your files more organized.

1. Click the "Finder" icon on your dock

2. Select "File"

3. Choose Folder

4. Enter the name of the folder you wish to use

5. Press the "Return" key button.

You can also create a new folder by clicking on the desktop, and from the pop menu select "New Folder", rename the folder with the name you wish.

How to take a screenshot

A screenshot is a picture of your screen, showing what is appearing on the screen at that exact moment. To take a screenshot you can use your keyboard's shortcuts or the "Screenshot" toolbar.

How to take a screenshot with keyboard's shortcuts

<u>Entire screen:</u> Press buttons: "Shift + Command + 3"

<u>To take a screenshot of a portion of your screen:</u> Press buttons: "Shift + Command + 4". Your pointer will change shape into a cross. Move it to where you want the screenshot to start and click and drag to select the area you want to be captured, release your mouse to capture the screenshot.

<u>To take a screenshot of a window:</u> Press buttons: "Shift + command + 4 + space bar". Your pointer will change shape into a camera. To take a screenshot of a specific window, move the camera above the window, click the mouse to confirm.

How to take a screenshot with "Screenshot" toolbar

1. Press buttons "Shift + command + 5"
2. The tools will appear on the bottom of the screen, above the dock.
3. The screenshot options are on the left side of the bar.

= [icon] Entire screen   [icon]   [icon] = Specific portion of the screen
= Window

All the screenshots taken will automatically save by default on the desktop, but you can move them at a later time on a different folder.

Make a video recording of the screen

Just like for the screenshot, you can also record a video of your screen, either for the entire screen or just a portion of it.

1. Open the built-in recording app "Screenshot" by pressing on the buttons "Shift + command + 5".

This tool bar will appear at the bottom of the screen, just above the dock, but you can move it around the screen where you prefer.

2. This option will allow you to capture a video recording of the entire screen.

This option will allow you to capture a video of a specific portion of the screen. You can resize the portion to your liking.

If you click on "Option" a menu list will appear that will allow you to select through different options such as where the video will be saved once you are done recording, if you want a timer to go off before the video starts recording, if you want to narrate throughout the video you can also select an option under "Microphone". *Remember the actual audio of the screen will not be recorded, to do so you will have to download a third-party application.*

3. Press on "Record" to start your recording.

4. Once done, and you want to stop the recording you can click the button on the top of the screen.

Your file will be saved where you have chosen to save it before recording the screen.

You can make calls from your computer through the built-in application "FaceTime", remember that FaceTime can only be used through Apple devices.

To make a call or videocall through FaceTime make sure:

1. You are connected through an Internet connection
2. You are logged in into your Apple ID.

To make a FaceTime call:

1. Go to your "Contacts" application
2. Search the person you want to call, either through a phone number or an email address
3. Click on the contact's profile
4. Select the option "FaceTime"

Receiving a FaceTime call on your MacBook:

1. You will receive a notification on your screen either as a pop-up window or on the top right corner.
2. You will be able to see the contact that is calling you
3. To take the call hit the "Accept" icon
4. To end the call hit the red icon

To make group Face Time calls on from your computer:

1. Open the "FaceTime" application
2. Select "New FaceTime"
3. Enter the contact details of all the people you wish to add to the group. Each contact must be separated by a comma. For example: Mark, Matthew, Anna
4. Click on the green icon to start the group call
5. You can also add people after the call has been initiated by clicking on the lower left corner of the FaceTime Group call window
6. The sidebar will appear, select "Add Person"
7. Select Add to invite the new component

Set up iMessage on your MacBook to send and receive text messages

 You can send and receive messages on your MacBook just as if you were using your phone, but you have to keep in mind that you can send and receive messages only within Apple devices. To set up the application:

1. Click on the "Message" icon

2. Sign into your Apple ID using your credentials

3. On the top left corner of your screen click "Messages"

4. Select "Preferences" from the drop-down menu

5. You can customize your settings according to your needs and preferences or select the account you want to use to run the application

To send a message

1. Click the button

2. Add the contact in the bar "To:", you can do so by typing the phone number, email, or the person's name (this will appear if saved in your contacts).
   You can also start a group chat by adding multiple names, remember that each name has to be separated with a comma

3. Type your text in the box at the bottom of the window, you can add emojis to your message by clicking on the emoji icon and selecting the one you wish to add from the menu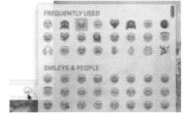

4. Once done, press the "Enter" key on your keyboard to send the message.

You will see all your conversation on the left side of the window, to view the entire conversation with a specific contact simply click on the person's name.

If you have an iPhone, you can also select to synch all your conversation to your MacBook. To do so:

1. Open the "Messages" app

2. Click on "Messages" at the top left corner of your screen

3. From the drop-down menu select "Preferences"

4. From the new window that will appear on your screen click on "Accounts"

5. Make sure that your phone number and e-mail address are selected under "you can be reached for messages at:"

6. From your iPhone go on "Settings"

7. Scroll down and select "Messages"

8. Select "Text Message Forwarding"

9. On the new window you should be able to see your MacBook listed

10. Tap the slider until it turns green to enable the forwarding feature

Now your text messages from your iPhone should begin to appear also on your MacBook.

How to automatically hide and show the menu bar

If you want to keep your desktop minimal you can choose the 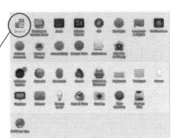 option to let the menu bar and dock.

To auto hide the menu bar:

1. Click on the Apple logo on the top left corner of your screen
2. Select "System Preferences"
3. From the menu select "General" on the top left corner of the new window
4. From the new window select on the box next to "Automatically hide and show the menu bar"

Your menu bar will automatically disappear and appear whenever you will hover your mouse on the top of your screen.

To auto hide your dock:

1. Right click on the title divider on the dock

2. In the window that will appear check the box next to "Automatically hide and show the Dock"
3. Once done click on the red button at the top left corner of the window

Your dock will automatically disappear and appear whenever you will hover your mouse at the bottom of your screen.

Use your emojis

Emojis can be used wherever there is a text box, so you can add an emoji on a message, an email, comment, etc.

To use the emojis you can use different ways, first make sure you are using an app that is notable (such as Messages, Notes, Word, etc):

1. Click "Edit" at the top of the screen
2. Select "Emoji & Symbols" at the bottom of the option list

1. You can use the keyboard shortcut by pressing Control + Command + Spacebar

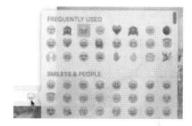

2. On "Message" you can simply click on the emoji icon

From the pop up window, you can scroll up and down to select the type of emoji you prefer.

If you click on the button on the top right corner you can expand the window and access the "character viewer" option. This will allow you to see the emojis better as they are bigger. You can search a specific type of emoji by typing in the search bar at the top right corner.

How to use the Mail application

 Before you can start using the Mail application on your MacBook make sure you are logged into your e-mail account.

You can use multiple email accounts at once, as we have already seen in the previous chapters.

How to send an e-mail

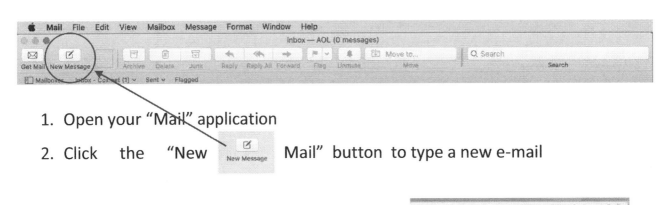

1. Open your "Mail" application

2. Click the "New Mail" button to type a new e-mail

3. Type the e-mail address on the first line (To:). You can add multiple contacts, each contact must be separated with a comma.

4. The Cc: line, if filled with a contact, allows you to send a copy of the e-mail.

5. Type the subject in the "Subject:" line, for example: "Staff meeting".

6. Type your e-mail/message in the message box.

7. To add an attachment such as a document, click the attachment button in the tool bar.

8. Once you are done click send at the top of your email.

As a standard, you will find the following mailboxes:

1. Inbox, where you will be able to access and read all the emails that you have received

2. Sent, where you will be able to read all the email you have sent

3. Drafts, where you can access the emails, you have started to write but have not finished or still have to send

4. Trash, where you can find all the emails that you have deleted

5. The "Junk" box is where all the emails considered to be "spam" are saved, you can open them at any time. Sometimes emails that are actually important might end up in the "Junk" box as they are automatically detected as potential spam.

Sign documents with your MacBook

Whenever we got a document that needed to be signed the best way used to be printing it out, sign it and then scan it. This can still be done, but there are easier and faster way to sign your documents directly on your MacBook without having to go through the usual lengthy process. You can digitally sign a document in "Preview".

1. Open a document in "Preview mode", normally that should happen automatically. In case it doesn't: press the key button "Control" and click on the document, from the drop down menu click "Open With" and then select "Preview". Let's pretend the document is asking for your name, the date and your signature.

2. Select the "Markup tool" ⊗ . Sometimes it might not appear as the window is not wide enough. In case it does not appear simply click the two arrows icon » , to be able to see more options, or widen the window.

3. From the tools that will appear select the "Textbook" tool .

4. A big sign "Text" will appear above the document with a default color and size.

5. To modify the style of the text click on and select the style, color, and size you want to use.

6. Type in the "Text" box your name

7. You can drag the text box with your name around by clicking and dragging the box and moving it to the place you want it to be.

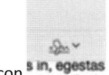

8. To add your signature click on the sign icon

9. Once clicked you can choose between different options to add your signature:

   a. It can be with the trackpad by drawing on it, once done press any key button

   b. With your camera (if you have it built in on your MacBook or have an external camera connected to the computer): you will first have to write your signature on a piece of paper, hold the paper to the camera in order to let it capture the signature, click "done" once finished.

Easy ways to share files from your MacBook

When it comes to sharing files there are several ways you can choose from. You can choose to share files by simply sending them as an e-mail attachment or through Bluetooth, but there are indeed other ways to do it. Let's them.

Through a folder

Choosing this way might come handy when there are different users using the same MacBook. Creating a folder means that you will be able to add inside of it several files each time you want to and will guarantee a quick and easy access to the other users that you will be sharing the folder to.

1. Create a folder, as we have seen in the previous chapters,
2. Select "System Preferences"
3. Select "Sharing"
4. On the left side of the new window, from the menu option, check the box for "File Sharing"
5. Now, on the box of "Shared Folders" you will want to add the folder that you want to share by clicking the "+" icon at the bottom of that same box
6. Find and click the folder you wish to share, once you are done click on "Add"
7. The "Users" box refers to the users of the same MacBook that will have access to that folder

You can decide what they can do with the files within the folder, for example be able to edit or just read, which means they will be able to open the files but not edit it. To change the actions

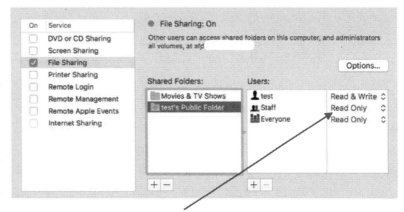

that the users can take simply click on above the "Read only" that will appear next to the user's name

8. Under the sign "File Sharing:" you will find the number that the other users will need in order to access the folder. Copy the number and send it either through e-mail or text.

Sharing files from MacBook to other Apple devices

1. You can use Airdrop, as we have already seen in the previous chapters
2. If you are sharing files between your Apple devices the best way to do it is by using iCloud.
   a. From your MacBook choose the file you want to share
   b. Copy and paste or move the file on iCloud drive in any folder you prefer
   c. You will be able to see the file on the same folder on iCloud from your other apple devices
3. Using the USB cable

a. Connect either the iPhone or iPad to the MacBook through the USB cable

b. Open "Finder"

c. In the side box of "Finder" you will see the connected apple device, for example: Gary's Phone

d. Click on the device connected

e. Move the file you want to share into a folder of the connected device

4. Through Bluetooth

a. Open "System Preferences"

b. Click on "Sharing"

c. From the menu option check on the box Bluetooth Sharing

d. Pair a device by going back to "System Preferences"

e. Select the "Bluetooth" icon

f. From the menu select the device you want to pair

g. Click on "Connect"

h. The other device will receive a notification that must be accepted in order to have a successful pairing

i. To send a file click on the file

j. On your keyboard press the keys Command + Shift + B

k. Click on "Run Service" on the pop up window

l. Double click on the device you want to send the file to

Crop, resize and edit your pictures

Pictures are stored in the "Photos" application, but this application, besides of having the function of saving pictures, is actually a great tool to edit your pictures as well.

1. Choose the picture you want to edit and open it
2. Click on the "Edit" button at the top left corner of the window
3. In this new window you will be able to edit your pictures, let's see the tools one by one:

This tool allows you to cut the picture, simply drag from any corner and drag until satisfied. Once you release the mouse, the picture will readjust itself but the part of the picture that's been cropped will still be visible under a dimmer light. You can drag the rectangle around the

Drag to enclose the area of the photo you want to keep.

Click to see the crop and straighten tools.

Drag to adjust the angle of the photo.

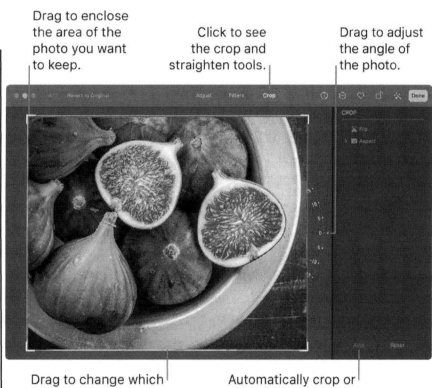

Drag to change which part of the photo shows.

Automatically crop or straighten the photo.

picture, if needed. If you change your mind, you can always click on reset at the bottom left corner to reset the picture to its original appearance.

Using this tool on the side of the picture (while on crop mode) you will be able to rotate the image.

By clicking on the "adjust" tool a new set of tools will appear on the side of the picture.

Every time you will make an adjustment by using any of these options you will see a blue button next to the option, if you click on it you will be able to see what the original picture looked like, click the dot again to readjust the new settings you've chosen.

By clicking on the undo button you will reset the picture to its original appearance. If you click on the triangle on the left side of the option, the option will expand. You can drag the line along to adjust the picture to your liking.

The filters option allows you to apply filters on your picture.

Once you are done editing the picture simply click on the button "Done" on the top right corner of the screen.

Family sharing work with sharing different things with family member up to six components. Family sharing allows you to share things like: Music, Applications, News, Tv, iCloud storage, and much more. This feature does not require to share the same Apple ID. The organizer will have to setup the "Family sharing" feature and will be able to invite the other five components, with their own Apple ID. The contents on the personal devices, such as messages, will not be shared. To setup "Family sharing" follow these steps:

1. Go to "System Preferences"
2. Click on "iCloud"
3. Select "Family Sharing"
4. From the menu you can choose the option you want to share with your family
5. Once you are done you can start inviting family members, click on the box "Invite Family Members".

Enable your keyboard on your screen

Enabling your keyboard on your MacBook's screen will allow you to see in front of you exactly what you are pressing on your keyboard. Sometimes it gets hard to type on your keyboard, especially if you are just getting started in the whole technological world. To enable your keyboard on your screen follow these steps:

1. Select the "Apple" logo on the top left corner of your screen
2. Click on "System Preferences"
3. On the window select "Keyboard" icon
4. On the keyboard window select on the "Input Sources"
5. In this tab check to box for "Show input menu in menu bar"

The input menu icon will not appear on your menu bar, click on it and on the drop down menu select "Show Keyboard Viewer" to enable the keyboard on the screen, you can type with your virtual keyboard by simply clicking on the letters through your mouse.

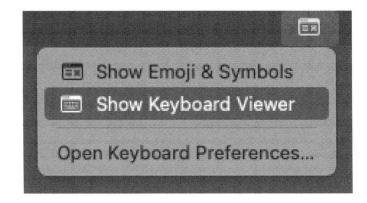

Change your conversation's name

If you are part of several group messages and you often get confused, you can easily rename the group message by following these easy steps:

1. Enter on the Message application
2. Select the group message you wish to rename
3. Select the "Info" icon
4. Tap on "Change name and photo"
5. You can enter the name by clicking on "Enter a Group Name"
6. Once you are done select "Icon"

Adjust your volume with smaller increments

When you tap on the keyboards to turn up or down your volume, this will change according to the default setting. If you find these changes too broad, you can adjust your volume with smaller increments.

When turning down the volume

1. Press on your keyboard: "Option" + "Shift" + the key button to lower down your volume.

To turn up the volume in smaller increments:

1. Press on your keyboard: "Option" + "Shift" + the key button to turn up the volume

Increase font size on your MacBook

To make it easier for you to read, you can increase the font size on your MacBook in different ways:

First method

1. Select the "Apple" logo on the top left corner of your screen
2. Click on "System Preferences"
3. Select "Display"
4. Select on "Scaled" and you can choose between the different sizes given from "Larger text" to "More Space"

Second method

1. From the "System Preferences" select "Accessibility"
2. From the option list select "Zoom"
3. Click on the box "Use keyboard shortcuts to zoom"
4. By using these keyboard shortcuts you will be able to zoom in and zoom out through a digital lens on a specific section of the screen.

From the same window

1. Check the box for "Enable Hover Text": by pressing the command key button you will have the text under the mouse enlarged.
2. By clicking on "Options" you can select the size on the font and other settings for the text.

Fourth method:

1. From "System Preferences" select "Accessibility"

2. From the option list select "Speech"

3. Click on the box for "Speak selected text when the key is pressed". Under the phrase you will also find the default key buttons to press in order for the computer to read out loud the text for you.

From the same window:

1. Select the box for "Speak items under the pointer"

2. This feature will let your computer read out to you the word underneath your pointer

Share your purchase with your family

You can share your purchases with your family, any time you want to, by using the "Family Sharing" feature. Let's see how you can share your new purchase with your family:

1. Tap on your "Apple' logo at the top left corner of your screen

2. Select "System Preferences"

3. Click on the family sharing icon, which normally can be found at the top right corner of the window

4. In the family sharing window select "Purchase Sharing" from the menu option

5. Click on "Set Up Purchase Sharing"

6. Click on "Share Purchase" on the new window to confirm the action

7. Follow the step by step guide that will appear on your window.

Change the source of your audio from your menu bar

There are different gadgets that can be used when it comes to audio. For example, you could be using some speakers or a headphone. Normally, when you connect an external device to your computer, this should automatically recognize the function of the device and work accordingly. But when, for example, you find yourself in need to switch from one output method to another, without disconnecting and reconnecting the external device, there are two different ways you can control it.

First method:

This method applies to macOS Big Sur and later

1. Click on the control center icon on the top right corner of your screen
2. Click on the arrow above sound
3. A new window will appear that will show you the different options you can select to have your sound coming out from. For example: from the MacBook's built in, if you have a speaker device connected you can choose to have the sound coming out from your speaker.

Second method:

1. Click on the "Apple" logo on the top right corner
2. From the drop down menu select "System Preferences"
3. Select the "Sound" icon
4. Select the "Output" tab
5. From the list you can choose the output you want to use for your sound
6. Click on the output you want to use
7. Once done simply click the red button on the top left corner to close the window

Clear your history search on Safari

To clear your Safari's history search:

1. Open Safari on your MacBook
2. On the menu bar click on "Safari"
3. Select "Clear History" from the drop down menu
4. From the pop up window you can select whether if you wish to wipe out all the history researches done so far on your MacBook or only the researches made on a specific time frame. *Remember: if you choose to delete all history, your saved pages and passwords will also be deleted from the Safari's memory.*
5. Click on the box "Clear History"

To clear specific sites from your history research:

1. Open Safari on your MacBook
2. On the menu bar select "History"
3. At the bottom of the drop down menu click on "Show Full History"
4. From the new window that will appear you can select specific site by checking the box next to the site
5. Once you are done selecting the sites you wish to delete simply click on the box "Delete" that can be found at the top right corner

Download from Safari

To download applications the best place is to always use the "App Store". But sometimes you might find yourself in need of downloading a file that is not available on the "App Store". In these cases, if you are going to download any type of file or application through Safari you need to always make sure you are downloading from the official page of the application as the chances to get viruses when downloading from Google or Safari are higher. To download from Safari:

1. On the website page you will normally be able to see a bight colored box and the writing "Download", click on the download box

2. The file will start downloading it and you will be able to see the progress of the download from the right top corner of the window

3. Once the download is done you can click on the file to open it or you can open the "Download" folder to open the downloaded file.

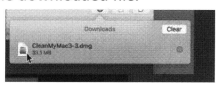

4. Open the file, if you downloaded an application a window will appear on your screen giving you instructions to follow, step by step, in order to properly install the application on your computer.

Run programs automatically as you log in into your MacBook

You have probably noticed that some applications on your MacBook open automatically as you start up your MacBook. Let's see why this happens and how to turn them off or let other programs run automatically as you log in into your MacBook.

Let's clarify first that when you are done working on your MacBook and simply close down your screen without completely turning off your computer, if you had applications running that you didn't close priorly, these same applications will pop-up as soon as you reopen your MacBook, as the computer was simply put to "Sleep".

When you restart your computer everything will start from zero, meaning, if you had applications running that were not closed before you restarted your MacBook these will be automatically shut-down. Some applications will start automatically as you log in into your MacBook. These, sometimes, can cause your computer to slow down. To disable the applications that startup automatically you can:

1. From the Dock right-click on the app
2. From the drop-down menu select option
3. Click on "Open at Login" if the check mark does not appear next to it anymore then you have successfully disabled the application from starting up automatically whenever you log in into your MacBook.

Another easier way:

1. Click on the "Apple" logo at the top left corner of your screen

2. Select "System Preferences"

3. Choose "Users & Groups"

4. Select on the "Login Items" tab

5. To remove an app select the application from the list and then click on the minus "-" button at the bottom of the box

To make an application automatically start when you log in into your MacBook

1. Click on the "Apple" logo at the top left corner of your screen

2. Select "System Preferences"

3. Click on "Users & Groups"

4. Select the "Login Items" tab

5. To add application to the startup click on the plus sign "+" at the bottom of the box

6. From the window search and select the application you wish to start automatically

7. Click on "Add' at the bottom left corner of the window

App switcher

The App switcher is the feature that allows you to switch from one application to another. To use the app switcher hold down the command key + press tab until you find the application you want to use, once you have found the application release the command key.

The "App switcher" application, other than switching between applications, can also deliver other tasks. For example you can hide or quit an application.

To hide:

1. Open the App switcher
2. Once you get to the application you want to hide while still holding the command key press the "H" key.

To quit:

1. Open the App switcher
2. Once you get to the application you want to quit while still holding the command key press the "Q" key.

THE NEXT STEP

How to use "Split screen"

Do you want to make the most of the screen space on your Mac or do you want to maximize it to its fullest? Split Screen is the correct feature, especially if you need to open multiple application on your screen, at once. You can use the Split screen feature to view two full-screen apps side by side and enjoy the convenience of utilizing two apps at once. This will be very convenient to do if you need to finish a work as fast as you can.

Here's how you can use split screen on your MacBook:

1. Hold the pointer over the full-screen green pointer button in an app window's upper-left corner.
2. When you click it, you'll be given the option of tiling the window to the left or right.
3. Choose which side of the screen the window should be on.
4. Choose which program windows you would like to utilize side by side.

If you're in a full-screen app, an alternative option to use the "split screen" is to:
1. Access Mission Control by double tapping the top of your magic mouse or scroll up with four fingers on your touchpad.
2. Drag any app onto the full-screen app's thumbnail.
3. To see the split screen completed, select the thumbnail of the full screen app.

To exit from your "split-screen" viewing mode, here is how to do it:
1. Move the pointer to the top of the screen to see the window buttons.
2. In either window, click the full-screen icon. Split View is now closed.
3. The other window expands to fill the entire screen.
4. You can utilize Mission Control to go to full-screen mode, and/or you can use a multi-Touch gesture like swiping left or right with four fingers on your trackpad.

Transfer images from your iPhone to your MacBook

Having the advantage of transferring photos gives you the benefit of utilizing your phone's storage in a better way. When it comes to sharing photos from your iPhone to your Mac, you have two options: use the photos app, image capture, or iPhoto, which is only available on the latest Mac OS versions.

Here's how to use image capture to import photos:

1. Select the spotlight icon , which is shaped like a magnifying glass, on your menu bar.

2. Type in "Image Capture".

3. After pressing the enter key, the app will launch.

The next step is to find the connected device.

4. Click on the device you want to connect in the devices section. If you have a lot of devices linked to your MacBook, make sure you click the right one.

5. On your chosen device, click on the image you want to migrate.

The next step is to choose a location for the photo. For example, you might want to put it on your desktop so that you can view it easily. This is how you can do it:

6. Select the photo and then select Desktop. Moreover, "Import" or "import all" are the two buttons available. If you wish to transfer a large number of photos, select Import All. If there is only one, you can click the import button.

7. When you select the photo and click Import, the photo will be transferred from your iPhone to your MacBook.

8. Close your image capture to see the picture that was transferred to your desktop.

Take note that the photo imported to your Mac will not automatically be deleted. However, on the other hand, you have the option to delete it. You can go to your iPhone and delete the photos you have already transferred to your MacBook and that could give you more storage space on your iPhone.

Customize file and folders icons

Customizing your files and folder icons is a unique way to put your desktop on a pleasing view. Furthermore, you organize it to whatever color or theme that you would want it to be, this way it will also be easier for you to find the folder or file each time you need it. File storage, as well as the tools you utilize to keep them organized, are important. While the most crucial step is clearly labeling files, so that you can quickly find what you need, a more visual method to immediately recognize what you need can also help you be more productive and efficient. Changing the folder symbol to a graphic, for example, allows users to find what you've been looking for immediately.

Another alternative is to replace these folders with a new color. Folder icons help distinguish the contents of a folder, while a different color can help identify the folder by type: music, movies, images, and so on. When used together, the possibilities are endless. And, if you ever feel like you've gone above and beyond with your classification system, you can simply go back to the original icon by pressing Command + X instead of Command + V.

You can customize your icons to whatever you wish, the only restriction is that they must be in PNG format. NPG is the acronym for: Portable Network Graphic (PNG) and it's a type of format in which pictures can be saved in. Because it can handle graphics with transparent or semi-transparent backgrounds, it's a popular file type among web designers. PNG files are commonly used to display high-quality digital images on websites. PNGs were created to outperform GIF files by providing not just lossless compression but also a considerably broader and brighter color palette.

To customize files and/or folder icon, here are the steps that you can follow:

1. Download the PNGs you'd like to replace in your folder.

2. Put all of your images in one folder to make it easier to find them.

3. Select a photo from the folder by clicking it.

4. To select everything in the photo, hit Command + A.

5. Then, to copy the photo, press Command + C.

6. Double-click the folder whose icon you wish to alter.

7. There would be a lot of options; choose show info, and a small icon of your folder will appear in the left corner.

8. You can modify in the head bar by slowly clicking it till it lights up.

9. The image should change if you paste or press Command + V.

Make sure you execute the Command + A step because many times it will not paste if you forget to do so. You could accomplish the same thing with desktop apps by following the same procedures, but you'd have to go to your Macbook's applications folder.

Create shortcuts from your keyboard

Having keyboard shortcuts can benefit you in a way that it is efficient. Using keyboard shortcuts instead of the mouse allows you to operate more quickly, efficiently, and precisely, saving you time and increasing your productivity. Keyboard shortcuts are also essential for persons with mobility or vision impairments.

On a Mac, you may give any menu item in any application a custom keyboard shortcut. You may even customize an app's default shortcuts. Having these shortcuts can make your life easier because you would not need to find it somewhere else but you can just easily type it. The first step is to write down the exact name of the menu item. For example, in Safari, there is a Bookmark option and a Show Bookmarks option. You must obtain the item's precise name, such as Show Bookmarks. The majority of products already have a keyboard shortcut assigned to them. You can, however, assign your own to those who don't. Here's what you can do about it:

1. Select keyboard from the system preferences menu.
2. Go to shortcuts at the top after clicking keyboard. A list of system keyboard shortcuts will appear.
3. Go to the app shortcuts. All of your custom keyboard shortcuts will be listed here.

So here's how you do it:

1. Enable the one-hit plus (+) button.
2. Select the program in which the menu item appears.
3. Enter the menu item's precise name. It is important to note that you must type the precise name with the exact spelling provided.
4. Then type the keyboard shortcut that appears after you click the application you want to use. A keyboard shortcut should consist of a modifier key combination followed by a regular key. Command, Option, Control, and Shift are modifier keys. (An example of a shortcut implemented is Command Option Control and the B key) In the keyboard shortcut bar, you'll see symbols representing each key.
5. Click Add when you've finished creating the keyboard shortcut. It will also show up on the app shortcut. You can alter it if you want to change the keys on your shortcut by clicking the keys on the left side of the menu item. You can also change the name of the menu item if you misspelled it.

To check, go to the application where you made the keyboard shortcut and look on the side of the menu item for the keys of the keyboard shortcut you created. And if it's not visible, it's most likely because you made a mistake.

Another piece of information is that if a menu item is disabled or grayed out, it will not work whether you select it from the menu or use a keyboard shortcut because it is not an active activity.

Another thing to keep in mind is that menu items may change names from time to time, but the good news is that you may add the keyboard shortcut using the same way. Every Mac user is unique. That is, one user may use certain programs while the other does not. This allows you to create custom keyboard shortcuts for the things that are important to you.

How to use your iPad as a second screen for your MacBook

"Sidecar" can now be enabled on your MacBook. You can utilize an iPad as an external display on a Mac with a Sidecar. There are no wires required; everything is done wirelessly using AirPlay. Unlike Universal Control, Sidecar does not allow you to use any files or programs on the connected iPad. Instead, the desktop of your Mac will be mirrored or enlarged on your iPad, allowing you to employ Multi-Touch gestures. You can even use the Apple Pencil while working in Adobe Photoshop on your Mac. For example, you could utilize the iPad as a Photoshop workspace, open a file in that workspace, and then edit the file with the Apple Pencil.

The iPad displays a Sidebar when using Sidecar to access modifier keys like Command, Option, and Shift. Sidecar additionally displays a Touch Bar at the top or bottom of the iPad that displays additional controls, similar to the actual Touch Bar on earlier MacBook Pros. To use this, your iPad must be running iPad OS and a compatible Mac must be running Mac OS Catalina. Here's how and what you can do about it:

1. In the dock of your MacBook, select System Preferences.

2. Sidecar is selected.

3. Connect your iPad by selecting it. Choose the iPad to which you want to connect. Once connected, the airplay icon will become blue, and you'll have a couple of options to turn off or on the sidebar and touch bar on your iPad at the bottom of the menu. The iPad sidebar places frequently used Mac controls on the side of the screen. It features modifier keys such as Command, Shift, and others, allowing you to select commands with your finger or Apple Pencil rather than a keyboard.

4. Is your **iPad** not visible, or is your Mac displaying an error message? Both your iPad and your MacBook should be restarted.

5. You can change the settings in this window if you want to. Your iPad can now be used as a second screen.

Close windows and apps from your MacBook that have been left opened on other apple devices

If you only use an app occasionally, you may want to quit it after you're done, especially if it consumes a lot of energy. And if it consumes a lot of energy from your mac, you might easily drain your battery. Apps that run in the background continue to drain your battery. If you're not utilizing a device, such as an SD card, Apple recommends detaching or ejecting it in order to save you battery.

Here is what you can do to close windows and apps from your MacBook to save energy:
1. Choose the App Name to close an app.
2. In the menu bar, select Quit App. For instance, Select Preview > Quit Preview (or press the keyboard shortcut Command-Q).

Keep in mind that clicking the Close button in the top-left corner of an app's window will close the window but not the app (a small dot beneath the app's icon in the Dock indicates that the app is active).

If for instance, an app is opened, such as Google, and you would want to close it, you can select the x on the upper left corner of the screen to close it. However, that does not stop there. Look closely below and you can see the icon right there with a dot on it indicating that it has not fully closed yet.

Alternately, you can do the following:

1. Beside the apple logo on the upper right corner of the screen, you would see the name of the app that you opened and wanted close. To close it, click the name of the app.
2. Click the last option given (Ex. Quit Google) and the app will automatically close and keep you from saving battery.

Connect your MacBook to the internet using your iPhone

To every Mac user there is, it is important for them to have an iPhone because they can easily have access to a personal hotspot. If you're working in a location where Wi-Fi reception is poor, you might wish to switch to a cellular network and connect using a personal hotspot to get a better internet connection. The standard procedure is to enable the hotspot in the phone's settings, then connect to it as a regular Wi-Fi network by inputting the password. Personal Hotspot allows you to share your iPhone's cellular internet connection with other devices. When other devices do not have internet connection through a Wi-Fi network, a Personal Hotspot is useful.

Note that not all providers offer Personal Hotspot. There may be additional charges. Your carrier and iPhone model determine the number of devices that can connect to your Personal Hotspot at the same time.

1. Tap Set Up Personal Hotspot in Settings
2. The tap on the bar next to Cellular.

Note: If Set Up Personal Hotspot is not an option and Cellular Data is enabled in Settings > Cellular, contact your carrier to add Personal Hotspot to your plan.

The following settings can be changed:

- Go to Settings
- Select Personal Hotspot
- You can select Wi-Fi Password to change your Personal Hotspot's Wi-Fi password.
- Disconnect devices and switch off Personal Hotspot by going to Settings
- Select Personal Hotspot
- Turn off Allow Others to Join.

Here's another option.

To connect a Mac or PC to your Personal Hotspot, you can use Wi-Fi, a USB connection, or Bluetooth. Choose one of the following options:

1. To connect via Wi-Fi on a Mac, go to the menu bar and select Wi-Fi status.
2. Then, from the list of the available networks select your iPhone.
3. Enter the password displayed in Settings
4. Select Personal Hotspot on your iPhone if prompted.

As long as your Mac is connected to your Personal Hotspot, the Wi-Fi status icon switches to the Personal Hotspot icon in the menu bar.

When you're signed in with the same Apple ID on your Mac and iPhone, and Bluetooth and Wi-Fi are turned on both devices, you can connect your devices to Personal Hotspot without entering a password.

Add a guest account on your MacBook

If you have numerous users on your Mac, you should create separate accounts for each of them so that they can customize their settings and choices without affecting the others. You can allow guests to log in without having access to other users' data or preferences. You can also establish groups that contain all of your Mac's user accounts. To complete these actions, you must be a Mac administrator.

1. Select the "Apple" logo on the top left corner of your screen
2. Select "System Preferences"
3. Click on Users & Groups. If the lock at the bottom left of the preference pane is locked, click it to unlock it.
4. Below the user list, click the Add button.
5. 4.Choose a type of user from the New Account pop-up menu.

There are three types of users:

Administrator: An administrator has the ability to add and manage other users, as well as install apps and adjust settings. When you first set up your Mac, you establish a new user who is an administrator. Multiple administrators are allowed on your Mac. You can make new ones and upgrade existing ones to administrators. For an administrator, do not enable automatic login. If you do, someone with administrator capabilities might just restart your Mac and obtain access. Don't share administrator names or passwords to keep your Mac safe.

Standard: An administrator creates standard users. Standard users can install programs and adjust their own settings, but they cannot add or edit the settings of other users.

Sharing Only: Sharing-only users can access shared files remotely but are unable to log in or modify computer settings. You may need to adjust settings in the File Sharing, Screen Sharing, or Remote Management panes of Sharing options to allow the user to view your shared files or screen. Set up file sharing and Share another Mac's screen for further information.

Click the Help button in the lower-left corner of the box for more information about the options for each user category.

1. Give the new user a full name. An account name is automatically generated. You can't alter your account name later if you use a different one.
2. Enter a password for the user, then double-check it. Enter a password hint to aid the user's password memory.
3. And then, create a new user.
4. You can also have any of the following, depending on what type of user you create:
    • Select "Allow user to administer this machine" for an administrator.
    • Select "Allow user to reset a password using Apple ID" for an administrator.
    • Specify whether the user can share your files and share your screen using Sharing options.
    After signing into your Mac or Magic Keyboard with Touch ID, a new user can add a fingerprint.

Mission control

When using your Mac, you may find that your screen is cluttered with a variety of apps and windows. This is especially troublesome if you're using a MacBook with a smaller screen than an iMac. Mission Control provides you with several desktops. In full screen or Split View, Mission Control provides a bird's-eye view of all your open windows, desktop areas, and any apps, making switching between them a breeze.

1. Use Control and Up Arrow to activate Mission Control or press F3 or hold down the Fn key and press F3 if you have a Mission Control shortcut. This activates Mission Control, and you can see that the first thing it does is separate all of the windows.
2. The Desktop is visible in the upper left corner. Click the plus button on the right side to add.
3. Move windows as many as you prefer to the added desktop to at least lessen the clutter there is on the first desktop.

Furthermore, you can switch between desktops using keyboard shortcuts. To switch between the two desktops, use Control and the left and right arrows. The Control Left Arrow will take you to the first desktop, while the Control Right Arrow will take you to the second.

You can also swiftly switch between desktops by using motions like four fingers on the trackpad and swiping left or right. This can be changed in system options, under trackpad and more gesture. You can make changes there. If your desktop is still cluttered, you can repeat the process by adding another desktop.

Update your MacBook

In general, it's best to keep your Mac up to date with software updates. Not only will you have access to the most recent features, but your Mac will also be protected against software defects and security breaches. Bugs, crashes, and even viruses are more likely on an old Mac. And if you wait too long for upgrades, your favorite apps may stop working entirely. It's a good idea to back up your Mac before you begin. Then, to identify and install any available software updates or upgrades, here are the following steps.

1. Click System Preferences from the Apple menu in the upper left corner of your screen.
2. Click Software Update in the System Preferences pane.
3. Click Update Now or Upgrade Now to get started.

When Software Update says your Mac is up to date, it implies mac OS and all of the products it installs, such as Safari, Messages, Mail, Music, Photos, FaceTime, and Calendar, are up to date as well. Updates for any apps you downloaded from the App Store can be found in the App Store.

Adding or removing a device to your MacBook

When you sign up for Apple services or purchase Apple products, the device you're using is immediately linked to your Apple ID. If you have two-factor authentication enabled on your Apple ID, deleting a device will prevent it from showing verification codes. It won't be able to access iCloud or other Apple services, like as Find My, until you check in with two-factor authentication.

You may want to uninstall a linked device in the following situations:

• If you've reached your maximum of device associations and wish to add another.

• If you are unable to re-download purchases made through the App Store, Apple TV app, iTunes Store, or other Apple services.

• If you wish to sell or give away a gadget that is connected to it.

To identify or remove your associated devices, use a Mac or PC.

Open the Apple Music app on your Mac. Alternatively, open iTunes for Windows on your PC.

1. Select Account.
2. Select Account Settings from your Mac's menu bar.
3. Choose Account
4. Select on View My Account from the iTunes menu bar on your PC. It's possible that you'll have to check in with your Apple ID.
5. Then select Manage Devices. This area will not appear if your Apple ID is not linked to any devices.
6. Remove a device by selecting the Remove button. If you're having trouble removing a device, sign out of your Apple ID and try again. If you still can't get rid of it, you may have to wait up to 90 days to link the device to a new Apple ID.

How to make a backup of your MacBook

Backups are important because if you unintentionally deleted all your files, there might still be a chance to recover them. However, if you don't do backups, the possibility that could happen is that when something goes wrong with your computer or it crashes or malfunctions ins some way, the risk would be losing all your data. On a macbook, you may be able to use the Time Machine, your Mac's built-in backup function, to back up your personal data, including apps, music, photographs, email, and documents, automatically. Having a backup allows you to restore files that you accidentally deleted or lost access to later.

1. Connect a USB or Thunderbolt storage device to your computer. Learn more about the backup disks that Time Machine supports.

2. Open the Time Machine options from the menu bar's Time Machine menu. Alternately, go to the Apple menu > System Preferences > Time Machine.

3. Select the backup disk.

4. Select your disk's name, then click Use Disk. Time Machine starts producing regular backups right away, without you having to do anything.

5. Choose Back Up Now from the Time Machine menu in the menu bar to start a backup manually rather than waiting for the next automatic backup.

6. Check the status of a backup or skip a backup in progress using the same menu. If a backup is in progress, the menu will reflect how much of it has been completed. When no backup is in progress, the menu displays the last backup's date and time.

Time Machine's advantage are the following:

- Time Machine backs up your data hourly for the last 24 hours, daily for the previous month, and weekly for all previous months. When your backup disk is full, the oldest backups are discarded. Although the first backup may take a long time, you can use your Mac while it is being done. Time Machine only backs up files that have changed since the last backup, making subsequent backups faster.

- Open Time Machine preferences, choose Options, then click the add (+) button to add an item to be omitted from your backup. Select an item, such as an external hard drive, and click the delete (−) button to stop it from being excluded.

- Hold down the Option key while selecting Browse Other Backup Disks from the Time Machine menu to back up multiple disks.

How to recover your files from a backup

If you back up your Mac with Time Machine, you can retrieve your files even if your system or startup drive is destroyed. This is the advantage of backing up your data because in case that there is an unintentional removal of the data, there is a way to recover it. It is important that before you can restore your files from your Time Machine backup, you must first reinstall mac OS on your Mac. If you're restoring your system due to an issue with your startup disk, make sure you fix or replace it before proceeding.

Make sure your Time Machine backup disk is attached and turned on before you begin. Make sure your Mac is connected to the same network as your disk.

1. Start your PC in recovery mode:
   • On a Mac with Apple silicon, go to Apple menu > Shut Down, press and hold the power button until "Loading startup choices" appears, then click Options, click Continue, and then follow the onscreen instructions.
2. Select Reinstall mac OS Monterey in the Recovery box, then click Continue to reinstall the version of mac OS saved on your computer's built-in recovery drive, including any installed upgrades.
3. Migration Assistant will ask if you wish to move data from another Mac or a Time Machine backup once mac OS finishes installing new system files. Click Continue after selecting Transfer from a Time Machine Backup.
4. Enter the name and password you use to connect to your backup drive if necessary. You may also be prompted to provide the password that was used to encrypt the backup.
5. Follow the onscreen instructions after selecting the date and time of the backup you want to restore.

How to remove a user account on your MacBook

Deleting or Removing a user account is important and beneficial not only when you want to deny someone access to your computer, but also when you create a user account on your own to try something out and then decide you don't need it. You can delete users who no longer need access to your Mac if you are an administrator. It is an easy process given that you are an administrator. Furthermore, you can also remove any unwanted groups.

The following are the steps on how to remove a user account on your MacBook.

1. On the top left side corner of your screen click on the "Apple" logo
2. Select "System Preferences"
3. Select "Users & Groups" from the menu
4. Choose the account or group you want to remove
5. Select the Remove button (a minus sign) underneath the user list. You won't be able to choose other users who are currently logged into this Mac.

6. Do one of the following:

    o   *Save the home folder as a disk image: Select "Save the home folder as a disk image," which preserves all of the user's documents and information for later restoration. The disk image is located in /Users/Deleted Users/.*

    o   *Don't alter the user's home folder: Choose "Don't change the home folder." The user's documents and information will be preserved, and the user can be restored if necessary later. /Users/ contains the home folder.*

    o   *Delete the user's home folder from the computer: Choose "Delete the home folder," which deletes the user's information and frees up storage space.*

    o   *Click OK to delete a sharing-only user or group.* A home folder is not available to a sharing-only user.

7. Then select Delete User.

Deleting a user account on Mac may saves all of the user's documents and information, allowing them to be recovered if necessary. The user's documents and information are preserved, and the user can be restored if necessary. The user information is removed, and storage space is made available.

Monitor: how to adjust your screen resolution

By default, your Mac selects the ideal display resolution for you. When using default resolution recommended to you, you can manually modify the resolution to make text and things appear larger on your screen, or to make text and objects appear smaller to free up more screen space. Knowing how to adjust your screen resolution based on your preference would give you comfort on using your computer. To do such things, you have to set a connected display's resolution. Additional resolution options are available after the monitor is connected if you have more than one display.

These following steps will guide you to adjust your mirror's resolution:

1. On the top left corner of your screen click on the "Apple" logo
2. Select "System Preferences"
3. Click on Display
4. Select "Display Settings"
5. From the sidebar chose your display, and then, depending on the display you have follow one of the following steps:

   • Select a scaled resolution for the display from the Scaled pop-up menu.
   • Select Scaled, then the resolution you'd like to utilize.

   You can also choose "Show all resolutions" to see additional display options
6. Select "Done" once you have finished.

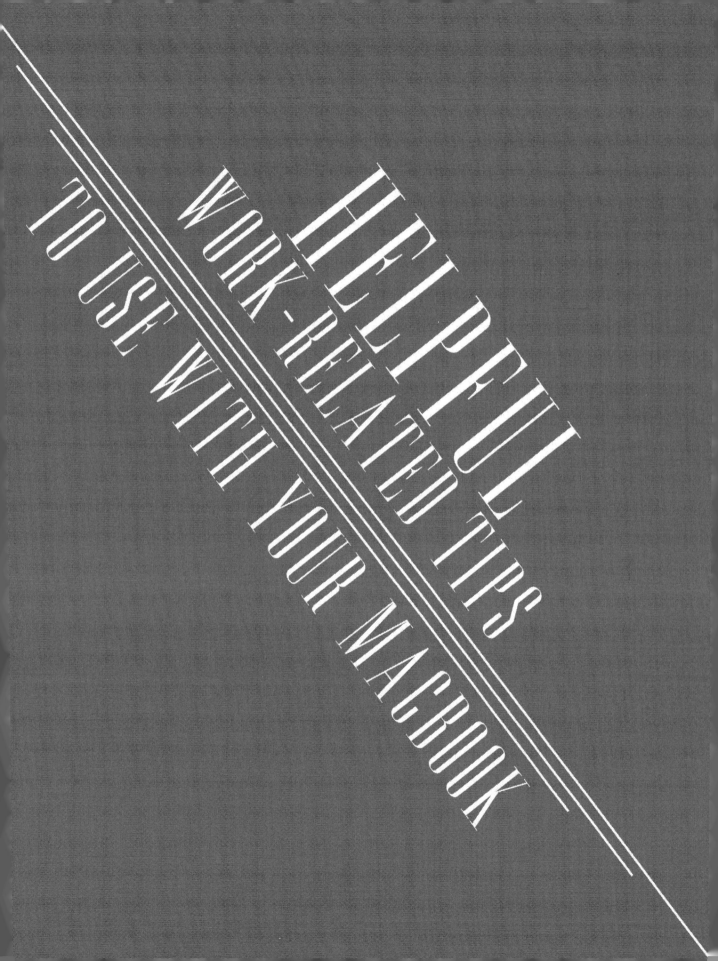

HELPFUL WORK-RELATED TIPS TO USE WITH YOUR MACBOOK

Use "Automator" to get things done quickly

Automator can be a little confusing when you are a first-time user, or just starting to get familiarized with this feature. Automator allows you to simplify those actions that you do often or repeatedly, and it can be used for different tasks on your MacBook.

1. Find "Automator" quickly by clicking on the spotlight and type in "Automator"

2. Open the "Automator" application

3. Allow the prompts you will be getting from your computer

4. Select "Workflow"

Once you will have access to this window you will be able to start creating a "script" of your action to carry out a specific task. (In this example let's pretend we are creating a script for picture editing)

1. Click on the "Finder" icon in the second box (shown in the image). This will make your computer start the task by looking in your computer.

2. Drag the "Finder" icon to the third box. Once the "Finder" application is dragged,

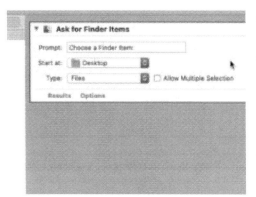

this is what the third box should show. You can customize the options, for example, if you click on "Start at" you can choose where the computer should search for the specific file (In this case could be the "Pictures" folder).

1. Click on "Run" at the top right corner of the window.

2. Choose a file from the list and click on "Choose" at the bottom right corner of the window.

3. The next step we will be taking for this example is copying the file we are going to edit. In the second box (as shown on the picture) type "Copy" in the search bar.

4. Select "Copy" from the list.

5. Drag "Copy" on the third box, as you did for "Finder".

6. Just like for the "Finder" you will have to customize and tell "Automator" where to copy this image.

7. The next step will be to tell "Automator" to resize the image, type on the search bar in the second box a keyword relating to the next action, for example, for resizing it will be "scale"

8. From the menu choose the correct option and drag it into the third box. You can customize this action through its designated box in the third part of the window (as shown in the picture)

9. Once you are done building the script of your action for "Automator" you can rename this process with the name you see fit and save it where it will be more easy for you without having to run "Automator" each time you want to do this action. To save and rename simply click at the top center of the window , as shown in the picture here below.

Remote access to a different screen

To remotely use or have access to another Mac's screen you will need to use "Screen Sharing". Before getting started you need to set up and configure the MacBook you want to have remote access to.

From the device you want to have remote control:

Start by enabling the MacBook to "Screen Sharing"

1. From the top left corner of your screen click on the "Apple" logo
2. Select "System Preferences"
3. Click on the folder "Sharing"
4. On the new window check the box next to "Remote Management"
5. In the second part of the window you can customize and select how many users you want to give access to on this device.
6. Under "Remote Management: ON" an IP address that you will need in

Remote Management: On

Other users can manage your computer using the address
‎.net.

order to access to this computer from another MacBook.

From the device from which you will be accessing from:

1. Open "Screen Sharing" application from the MacBook. Since it is not among the usual applications and finding by manually searching through each folder can be a daunting task, the easiest solution is to use "Spotlight" and type in the search bar "Screen Sharing" .

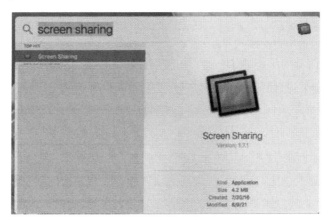

2. Type in the IP address you previously got from the computer you want to access to, while setting "Screen sharing" up.

3. Once done click on "Connect"

4. Type in the credentials in the new window

5. Click on "sign in"

On your screen will appear the MacBook's screen you have access to. From here you can carry out any task you want.

iCloud Drive

 iCloud Drive is a location where you can safe your files, to which you can have access from multiple Apple device through the same Apple ID. Using "iCloud Drive" to store your files in is also a great way to save space on your computer that way it will not start running slow. To use your iCloud Drive:

1. From the top left corner of your MacBook click on the "Apple" logo

2. Select "System Preferences"

3. Click on you Apple ID

4. Select iCloud

5. Turn on your iCloud Drive if it's off

6. Choose "Desktop & Documents Folders"

7. Click on "Done" once you are finished

Better alternatives to send large dimension files

When sharing files we can use several ways to send them to someone, and most of the times bigger sized files are easy to send. The only application you might find restriction with is when you are sending attachments via email. Here we will uncover other alternatives to send larger size files.

1. If you are trying to share a large size image, you can share it through iCloud Photo Gallery.

    a. Go to the photo application from your MacBook, select the picture or the pictures you want to share.

    b. Click on the share button

    c. From the drop down menu select "Share Albums"

    d. Click on the plus sign "+" to create a new shared album.

    e. From the drop down menu you can customize the album and invite people to be able to see what is in the album

2. You can share files through iCloud Drive. (To use this alternative make sure your iCloud Drive is turned on)

    a. Select the file you want to share by pressing on "Control" and then clicking on the file

    b. Select "Share"

    c. From the drop down menu select "Share People"

    d. Select the Option you want to use to share the file

Create a partition of external hard disks

To create a partitional for an external hard disk:

1. Open "Spotlight"

2. Type in the bar "Disk Utility" and then click on the latter.

3. On the top left corner click on "View"

4. Select "Show All Devices"

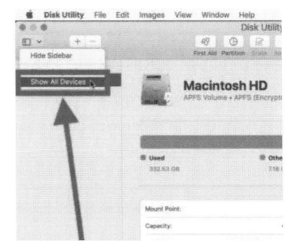

5. From the list that will appear select the external hard drive

6. From the menu bar click on "Edit"

7. From the drop down menu select "Erase"

8. Once done you can customize the partition by clicking on "Partition" at the top of the window

9. On the new window you can add a partition by clicking on the plus sign "+" and use the slider to adjust the size of the partition.

10. Click on "Apply" at the bottom right corner.

Firewall

One of the greatest feature of the Apple devices revolves around the built-in features that help to stay protected from external and viruses attack. When surfing around the Internet, downloading files, opening attachments, etc., the chances of getting attacked by viruses are high. This is a common problem with Windows computers. To keep a Windows computer safe from these external attacks one must have an anti-virus software, which rarely comes free and most of the times to have a decent protection system also means an extra expense. Apple devices, though, are harder to get attacked by viruses because of the built-in features, but an extra precautionary step can only bring benefits, especially if we were to consider the prices these computers are sold for. In this case the best option is to turn on the firewall in your MacBook. A Firewall is a network security that filters all the traffic coming in and going out of your computer, imagine a wall that divides your device from the external and public Internet. The benefits that come with the an activated Firewall are several which include:

1. Monitoring of the incoming and outgoing Traffic.
2. Stop possible virus attacks from external sites
3. Prevents hacking
4. Stops spyware (which are software that get downloaded on our computer without our knowledge, while surfing the Internet or downloading a different application)
5. Higher protection of your privacy

To turn your Firewall on:

1. Click on the "Apple" logo at the top left corner of your screen

2. Select "System Preferences"

3. In the window click on "Security & Privacy"

4. In the new window click on the "Firewall" tab

5. Turn on the Firewall by clicking on the dot next to "Firewall". Once it turns its color in green your Firewall will be on and the text next to it will also inform you that is on.

Filevault

Filevault is a built in system with the task of encrypting the MacBook's disk. Its main role is to encrypt all the data that can be found in the computer's hard disk in order to make them accessible only to the owner or the user with authorization, thus, to protect from external attacks that might gather some of your important information.

To turn on your Filevault:

1. On the left top corner of your MacBook click on the "Apple" logo
2. Select "System Preferences"
3. Select "Security & Privacy"
4. In the new window click on the tab "Filevault"
5. You might come across to the possibility that the box you need to click on in order to turn the "Filevault" on is in a dimmed grey color, therefore can not be clicked. In this case you will have to click on the lock you can find on the bottom left corner of the window. Insert your credentials. After this operation you should be able to click on the box "Turn On Filevault".
6. Click on the box "Turn on Filevault" :
   You will have two options:
   a. Allow the iCloud account to unlock the disk. In case you forget your password to your computer, you can unlock your desk through your iCloud account.
   b. Create a recovery key. You will be prompted, on your screen, a string of numbers and letters. Make sure to write it down and store it in a safe place, that is not your computer, in order to be able to use it in the future in case you forget your password.

This process may require some time to turn on, according to your computer.

A negative aspect about turning your Filevault on is that this might cause your computer to run a little slower.

MOST COMMON ISSUES ONE MAY ENCOUNTER WHILE USING A MACBOOK AND HOW TO FIX THEM

We have established that switching to a MacBook is one of the best ideas, when it comes to computer devices. Although the prices are pretty high you get the value of your money, but they are not immune to issues. Here we will go through some of the most common issues you might encounter and how to fix them to get you back on the ground.

Issues starting up your MacBook

If your computer is having trouble starting and you find yourself in front of a gray screen, instead of your desktop, you can reboot your MacBook in "Safe Mode". This will allow your computer to restart by using the bare minimum of the software and will do automatic repairs to your directory, in case there is any issue that is causing your MacBook to not run properly.

1. Turn on you MacBook
2. Press and hold the "Shift" key.
3. You can release the key button once the Apple logo appears.
4. Once done restart you MacBook as usual.

Unresponsive applications

You might be working on an application and all of a sudden it freezes, and you are not able to take any further actions. You can Force Quit the application to let it restart and open it again.

1. Click on the "Apple" logo on the top left corner of the screen
2. Select Force Quit Or Press the key buttons: Command + Option + Esc

3. On the window select the application that is not working and click on the "Force Quit" button

You MacBook dies suddenly

If your MacBook is shutting down there could be different reasons to why this is happening. First make sure your battery level is enough, if not connect the computer to the charger. If that's not the case, you can:

1. Restart your MacBook by using the power button
2. Restart once again the computer. This will allow your MacBook to do a healthy shutdown.
3. Once your screen is back on reset your System Management Control. This will fix any possible issue in your computer.

If this procedure does not fix your problem, contact the Support Center or head to the nearest Apple Store, the problem might be something else that only a technician can solve.

Troubles connecting other devices to your MacBook

If you are trying to connect a device to your MacBook and it's not connecting properly, first, make sure the chord is plugged in correctly and in the correct port. Make sure the cable is not damaged. If it is still not working you can:

1. Restart your MacBook
2. Restart the device you are trying to connect to your computer.

If the devices are still not connecting it might simply be because they are not compatible, therefore they can not be connected to each other.

Continuous flickering of the screen

Sometimes you might notice that your screen starts to dim or lose resolution in repeated and rapidly sequences. The main cause for this issue is that your physical screen might have undergone some damages, in this case you will need a complete screen replacement. If your screen does not have any physical damage, try to restart your MacBook, or alternatively you reset the PRAM or NVRAM:

1. Press the power button on your MacBook

2. Hold these key buttons at the same time: Command + Option + P + R

3. Keep pressing the keys until your Mac restarts a second time.

Your camera's resolution is poor while on FaceTime

You notice that your camera's resolution is low while on Facetime, but when you switch to the camera's application the resolution is fine? The problem might not be with you camera. First make sure your camera is clean and that nothing is obstructing it. If the problem persists then the issue might be with the FaceTime application, check if there is any update that needs to be done, that might be the issue.

Slow MacBook

If you noticed that your MacBook is running slower than usual, in most cases it might be because you are running too many applications at the same time. Try closing the applications you are not using. Try to move some of your files (such as videos or images) on an external memory device or on iCloud and erase them from the computer, this will free up your computer's memory space and will start running faster. Alternatively check if there is a Software Update that must be made, having an older version of the software may be the reason for your MacBook to be so slow.

Battery draining fast

A battery that is draining very quickly can be related to many different reasons, sometimes, if you don't need to change the battery, you can take some actions. First, if you have many applications open, close the ones that you don't need. Or:

You can reduce the motion

1. On the top left corner of your screen click on the "Apple" logo
2. Select "System Preferences"
3. Select Accessibility
4. Click on "Display"
5. Check the box for "Reduce Motion".

By reduce the motion you will, considerably, consume less battery.

Overheating and loud noises

If your MacBook is heating up and feels too hot to the touch, as simple as it sounds, make sure to put the computer in a position where there is enough space to let air pass. Avoid keeping your computer on a cushion as this is going to block the air vents.

Unresponsive MacBook

If your MacBook becomes unresponsive and you don't want to wait, the best solution to this issue is to restart your computer.

1. Press and hold the power button until the screen turns off
2. Wait a few seconds, to let the MacBook cool down and then turn it back on by pressing on the power button.

The MacBook's sound suddenly goes off

If you are having this kind of issue, first, if you are using a specific application make sure the issue is not within that app. Try opening a different application and test your audio out, if it's now working then the issue is not with your computer, but most likely with the app. It might needs to be updated or there might be a bug. If the issue persists, and is happening with all the other applications as well, if you are using an external device (such as an earphone or a speaker) make sure they are working. First of all, switch the resource of the audio's output to your internal speakers, if it's working then the problem is most likely with your external devices, make sure they connected properly. Another fix is by trying to set your PRAM/NVRAM and SMC:

1. Press the power button on your MacBook
2. Hold these key buttons at the same time: Command + Option + P + Keep pressing the keys until your Mac restarts a second time.

If the problem still persists the issue might have to do with the hardware, in this case the best solution is to refer to a technician.

Your MacBook will not shut down

If you are having some issues shutting down your computer while your MacBook is unresponsive, an open application might be preventing your computer from shutting down. The best solution is to Force quit all the frozen apps. If the issue is persistent, try to fix it by resetting the NVRAM to see if it helps.

1. Press the power button on your MacBook
2. Hold these key buttons at the same time: Command + Option + P + Keep pressing the keys until your Mac restarts a second time.

Your MacBook is not charging while plugged in

Start with the most obvious solution: check that your charger is properly plugged in to the computer and to the power source. Second, make sure your charger is not damaged, this is one of the most common issue why a MacBook is not charging although plugged to the power source. If the problem persists press down the Option key and click on the battery icon on the menu bar at the same time. By doing this, you will have access to advanced options of your battery. The menu might suggest you that there is a problem with the physical battery and that it needs to be replaced.

The Bluetooth is neither turning nor turning off

If you are having issues turning on or turning off your Bluetooth:

1. On the top left side corner of your screen click on the "Apple" logo
2. Select "System Preferences"
3. Choose Bluetooth

Sometimes turning on or off your Bluetooth from this window, instead of using the shortcut on the menu bar can be the solution.

If the problem still persists the issue might be your Software that is too old, try updating your MacBook and then check if by updating the computer your issues is fixed.

Another solution can be manually rebooting your Bluetooth:
1. Type the command: "sudo rm - /Library/Preferences/com.apple.Bluetooth.plist"
2. Press the enter key button on your keyboard
3. Select Enter once again after typing in your credentials, if required.
4. Restart your MacBook.

TERMINOLOGY

Here you will find the explanation of the terms you will find yourself crossing path with a lot of times.

Software = a software is the program or programs, set of instructions and data that are used by the computer to carry out specific tasks.

Hardware = hardware, when it comes to technological lingo, indicates the physical components of a device.

Application / App = a mobile or device application, most commonly referred to as app, is a type of software that runs on a device that provides different type of services. For example messaging service, such as Whats App.

MacOS = MacOs is the operating system of every Mac. MacOS is designed to be used only on an Apple computer.

Browser = a browser is a program that allows you to interact with the Internet and all of it's information, such as Web pages, videos, images, songs, movies.

Gigabyte or GB = a gigabyte is a unit made of data and is typically used to indicate storage capacity.

Icon = an icon, when it comes to a computer or a phone, is an image that graphically represents the application, the file, or the folder.

Desktop = the desktop is the computers display where documents, files, images, and applications can be found.

CPU = CPU stands for Centra Processing Unit, is the component of a computer that controls the interpretation and execution part of the device.

GPU = GPU stands for Graphics Processing Unit and it specializes in rendering images or videos on a device's screen.

RAM = RAM stands for random-access memory. When talking about RAM in a computer we refer to the short term memory, where the data is being processed.

Storage = a storage, like in normal life, is the designated area where we store our data. It can be internally in our computer, digitally such as iCloud or an external device designated specifically only in storing data.

Emoji = emoji or emoticon are popular pictures used in messages to express emotions.

SHORTCUT TABLE

To make your life easier and be able to carry out tasks in a faster manner this table will definitely come in handy.

COMBINATION	FEATURE
Command + Shift + 3	Screenshot the entire visible window.
Command + Shift + 4	Screenshot a specific area of the screen.
Command + Shift + 5	To open and see all the screenshot tools
Command + H	Hides applications
Command + X	To cut the selected item
Command + C	To copy the selected item
Command + V	To paste the item you either copied or cut
Command + Z	To undo the command you just carried out
Command + A	To select all items
Command + F	To find an item in a document
Command + F	To open the Find window
Command + G	To find an item
Command + M	To minimize the front window to the Dock
Option + Command + M	To minimize all the windows to the Dock
Command + O	To open the selected item

Command + P	To print out the current page you are in
Command + S	To save the document you are current in
Command + T	To open a new Tab, for example, on Safari
Command + W	To close the window you are currently in
Option + Command + Esc	Force quit an application
Command + Space bar	To open "Spotlight" and quickly find an application, file, folder, data, etc.
Control + Command + Space bar	Will open the emoji window to a wider one from where you can choose the right emoji or symbol
Control + Command + F	To open the application to full screen
Command + Tab	To switch to another one, to the most recent you just used
Shift + Command + N	To create a new folder in the Finder
Command + comma button (,)	To open preferences
Option + Command + Power Button	To put the computer to sleeping mode
Control + Shift + Power Button	To put your screen to sleeping mode
Control + Power Button	To open a window in which you can select if you either want to restart, put to sleep or shut down your MacBook.
Control + Command + Media Eject button	To quit all the apps you have opened

Control + Command + Q	To lock your screen
Shift + Command + Q	To log out from your computer's user account
Command + D	To create a copy of the selected files
Command + E	To eject the disk
Command + F	To start a spotlight search in the Finder
Command + I	To show the Get Info window of a selected file
Shift + Command + F	Open the "Recents" window
Shift + Command + I	To open iCloud Drive
Option + Command + L	To open the "Downloads" folder
Shift + Command + R	To open the AirDrop window
Option + Command + D	To show or hide the "Dock"
Command + N	To open a new "Finder" window
Command + Delete	To move the specific selected file in the trash bin
Option + Shift + Command + Delete	To empty the trash bin
Option + Volume up	To open the "Sound" window to customize the volume
Command + B	To change the text's font into **Bold**
Command + I	To change the text's format into *Italic*
Command + U	To underline the text

Command + ;	To show and find possible misspellings in the document
Command + Up Arrow	To move the pointer to the end of the document
Command + Down Arrow	To move the pointer to the beginning of the document
Command + Right Arrow	To move the pointer to the end of the current line
Command + Left Arrow	To move the pointer to the beginning of the current line

Conclusion

Getting familiarized with technology can be intimidating, especially when things are moving as fast as they are today. But keeping up with what is around us is always a good idea, especially when most of the daily tasks are done through phones or computers. It's normal to tend to choose for the cheapest option, especially when you are looking to buy a new computer, but most of the time spending those extra couple of hundreds are going to save you more along the way, especially because of the quality of the product. With this guide you will be able not just to get started with your MacBook, but also get more familiarized with it and learn tricks that will help you when it comes to managing your files.

Printed in Great Britain
by Amazon

15541273R00084